Soul S

A Short Course Exploring Prayer and Spiritual Growth

Nick Helm

Bishop of Sheffield's Advisor in Spirituality

GROVE BOOKS LIMITED
RIDLEY HALL RD   CAMBRIDGE   CB3 9HU

Contents

Acknowledgments

This booklet owes a great deal to the support and work of Angela Brown. She has played a significant part in running Soul Spark since its early days and has contributed appreciably to its shaping and content. Many thanks to her and to the many who have been part of the teams that have run the course. I am grateful to those who have participated and shared their journeys and reflections with me as I have prepared this booklet. Thanks also to Roly Riem who helped refine my rather loose writing! Last but by no means least, thanks to my wife Pat for her support, encouragement and help.

The Cover Illustration is the logo used by 'Soul Spark'

First Impression February 2006
Reprinted April 2008
ISSN 0262-799X
ISBN 1 85174 615 3

Introduction

'My relationship with God has been enriched, giving me a renewed sense of my purpose in life.'

'I have come through [Soul Spark] wiser and with a dream: not I, but we, the Lord and I. The journey has just started and my life must undergo changes.'

'The experience as a whole has helped me to practise slowing down in prayer and not approach it so much as a job of work.'

These are not untypical comments from people at the end of the Soul Spark course. They give glimpses of grace at work and testify to a course which seeks to 'allow the creator to deal with the creature.'[1]

The processes involved in this course have transformed many participants' faith journeys as well as enriching those running the course. Aware of the power of God at work, we sense a continuing invitation to share it with others.

How to run Soul Spark? In this booklet we explore and share:

- *Understanding spirituality and the three keys to spiritual growth* that have shaped the course in chapters 2 and 3.
- *Detailed plans* for each of the six sessions with guidance on holding the process and content are in chapter 4.
- *Guidance* on preparation, running and leading Soul Spark is in chapter 5.
- *Resources and handouts* beyond the scope of this booklet are available for download from the internet at www.course.soulspark.org.uk

This course requires a commitment to a profound process. Those who run this course need to engage with it and let their involvement be part of their own spiritual journey. The impact of the course is more significant when led in this way. It will also preserve the course's purpose and integrity.

2

Soul Spark—The Course

'What about a course for the rest of us?' asked someone not wanting to do our introductory course on Spiritual Direction.

As this resonated with several other nudges, we took the step to shape a course that would offer something to anyone seeking to explore Christian spirituality in a real and practical way. We aimed to create a series of sessions, with the experiential approach of the Spiritual Direction course, using some of its key features. Since the original course in Rotherham in 2000, it has been held in various settings in South Yorkshire and has had a positive reception.

The name of the course, Soul Spark, comes from Meister Eckhart's image of the 'Spark in the Soul' and the idea that this spark can be fanned into flame. Importantly this needs time and attention. Soul Spark gives an opportunity to attend to soul life, to dispose oneself to the Spirit of God, to pray, to reflect, to share, and explore perspectives on the dynamics of the spiritual life.

> Soul Spark seeks, in six two-hour sessions to:
> - Broaden approaches to prayer by introducing various ways of praying.
> - Develop a more reflective and discerning approach to spirituality and life.
> - Offer helpful perspectives to make more sense of the spiritual life.

The approach is experiential rather than didactic. It uses a model that is different to Bible study and discussion groups, prayer groups, teaching courses and other more common approaches used in church life. It seeks to foster spiritual experiences rather than providing head knowledge. Rather than talking about prayer and God and hoping that some of this touches people, the starting point is prayer; to pray and notice the effect this has. It encourages prayed rather than taught theology, which is personally involving and transforming.

The process of the course can seem benign, gentle and warm and leave people with their own choices. However, I doubt if anyone who has experienced Soul Spark would describe it as undemanding and unchallenging. It asks much of people to engage in approaches to prayer and listening to one another that may not come naturally. What keeps people on board is their own inner desire to explore their relationship with God further. What challenges and changes them more than anything is encountering God in their prayer and reflection.

This is not a course for everyone. Almost always people drop out, because they do not find it 'scratching where they are itching' or do not find the process suits, but many persist and are glad to have done so.

Course Outline

	Prayer Exercise	Topic for Reflection
Session 1	Praying with Scripture: Lectio Divina	Approaching Spirituality
Session 2	Reflection Exercise	Journeying with God
Session 3	Praying with Scripture: Imaginative Contemplation	Who am I?
Session 4	Visual Contemplation	God of Grace
Session 5	Healing Prayer	Called to Become
Session 6	Poetry	Journeying on…

Session Plans

All sessions have the same basic structure, though the first and last are adapted to suit the particular needs of beginning and ending the course. The session has three roughly equal parts. The timing needs holding lightly, but not too loosely.

Welcome, Introduction and Check-in	10 mins
Stilling and Prayer Exercise	30 mins
Listening Groups	25 mins
Reflection on Listening Groups	7 mins
Input—reflections on subject	25 mins
Final reflection	10 mins

The detailed session plans in chapter 4 give further breakdown of the structure and suggestions, guidelines and other details for handling the different parts of each session through the course.

We strongly encourage taking this material and enriching it with reflections from personal experience.

The course web site www.course.soulspark.org.uk has resources for downloading. These include all the handouts, the prayer exercises, background material for the talks and follow up exercises. Permission is given for printing and copying for use in running a Soul Spark course.

3 Spirituality—Keys to Growth

The growth in interest in spirituality has brought with it a mystique that arouses both attraction and suspicion.

What is it that we are really talking about? Is it not just self-indulgent navel-gazing? What can give me a deeper meaning to my life? Any course exploring spirituality needs to begin by setting out how it is understood and how this underpins the process of the course.

One way of understanding spirituality is in relation to Jesus' response to the question 'What is the greatest commandment?' His response was 'Love God…and love your neighbour as yourself.'

Spirituality is about relationships to:

- God—in prayer, worship and the way life is lived.
- Oneself—relating to personal and inner awarenesses.
- Others—relating, responding and engaging with the rest of humanity and creation.

Christian spirituality is about living this out, finding the resources and making the choices that result in more healthy living out of these relationships. What helps such growth? What helps each of us becoming who we were created to be? To be more truly oneself is to be more truly who God created us to be, and therefore to live out more fully one's calling. Attentiveness to these matters of the inner life cannot be navel gazing, but rather the foundation of discipleship.

Understanding spirituality in this way has implications for all of life, setting it at the heart of our identity and mission. It is not an added on extra to enhance life, an otherworldly dimension, but rather is about being fully human. It is the food of life—without which life is impoverished. People have more spirituality in their life than they often realize (even among those who do not affirm a faith or acknowledge their own spirituality). However, it also gives recognition to the deep longings in lives. At their deepest these are God given and pointers to each person's unique calling. They can also be pointers to the need for healing where life has damaged and distorted that calling.

We have many choices in life. These include:

- how we live our life
- how we respond to the chosen and unchosen that happens to us
- what we draw on for support, encouragement and resourcing

Discernment lies behind the choices. On what basis do we make a choice? What do we listen and respond to in the clamour of voices (inner and outer) that seek to influence the choice we make or do not make? This is where one's spirituality affects life in a significant and practical way.

Taking one's spirituality seriously is potentially radical and subversive. It holds the possibility of growth into greater spiritual freedom to faithfully follow the call of Christ in one's life, and therefore to live out the radical and subversive gospel of Jesus Christ.

All this needs a safe space where there is freedom to be oneself, to pray, to reflect, to share, to be listened to. These are the ingredients necessary to discern the movements of the Spirit and to respond to them. Soul Spark seeks to provide them. This is not as easy as it sounds, for being human, as we seek to offer the course, we can be tempted away from the process. This brings its own growth points. Soul Spark thus becomes a journey for its leaders as well as its participants.

Three Keys to Spiritual Growth

The three key elements that make up a session are:

- *spiritual exercises* (prayer, but also activities that may not be immediately recognized as prayer)
- *reflection* on the experience and on the spiritual life (this involves both individual reflection and reflections offered by a team member)
- *personal sharing* with others about the experience (in small groups)

They are seen in every Christian spiritual tradition. Experience has shown that by these processes we can be more open to discern God's Spirit and be led in taking significant steps of faith.

Spiritual Exercises

We use the term 'spiritual exercise' to suggest something much wider than that which is usually evoked by the word 'prayer.' Spiritual exercises are activities that have an intentional purpose to be open and attentive to God. They may involve words and thoughts, but also images, imagination, reflection and self-awareness. All this and more is prayer.

Prayer is a dynamic relationship with God. To pray is to let the Holy Spirit pray in us. It is primarily an inner disposition, rather than action or activity. Instead of saying much about this through the course, we simply let experience be the teacher, and allow the shifts in perceptions of prayer to emerge and be noticed.

Preparation for prayer is important. Giving too little time to preparation often results in a struggle to enter deeper prayer. We offer stilling/relaxation exercises as a means of preparation, of disposition. In itself this preparation is prayer, seeking to be open to God and to entrust oneself, one's fears and burdens to God so they do not get in the way.

There are innumerable ways of praying. Each of us has particular and individual ways of engaging our spirit with the Spirit of God. Nevertheless there are some significant common ways valued by many in the Christian tradition. We have struggled to whittle it down to six, but have opted for approaches that are about receiving from God. These include using scripture in prayer with lectio divina and imaginative comtemplation, reflection exercises and using Christian art and poetry.

Reflection

Socrates famously stated that the unreflected life is not worth living, and there is a truth in his statement. However, giving time and finding focus for reflection is not always easy. 21st century life has an inbuilt movement to action and activity rather than reflection. Church life and worship can often collude with this tendency to avoid reflection and discernment. Creating space and offering focus for these reflections lie at the heart of the process of each session.

The felt experience of prayer and reflection is significant to the discerning of God's leading. There is often a tendency to focus on the more 'heady' questions of doctrine, biblical criticism and interpretation or to trying to generalize from individual experience. So we often need gentle encouragement to pay attention to the underlying inner experience. It is in attending to this inner response we begin to discern God's movements. Once this awareness has emerged it can be valuable to stay with the feelings and gently reflect on them and what they are revealing. This enables the transforming work of the experience to develop and deepen. It is an inside out process and contrasts with many 'teaching' models.

The third part of each session offers a wider perspective for reflection. Drawing on the wider Christian tradition, as well as personal experience, there is an opportunity for participants to set their experience in a broader context. While this can look like 'teaching' it needs to be more of an 'offering' with the invitation to notice what is helpful and connects with their experience. They can take what is helpful and leave what is not, perhaps picking up on it later when it becomes relevant.

We also encourage participants to keep a journal, making notes of their experience and reflections on it. They are invited to do this at various points through the sessions, as well as at home. This leads to further insights and deeper awareness and aids choosing how to respond to God.

Sharing

Sharing faith experience is an important part of Soul Spark. It can arouse strong and seemingly conflicting responses. Many find it both the hardest and the most valuable part of the course. The listening groups become places where often things are shared that have never been shared before.

In small groups, members are invited to share something of their experience of the prayer time, while all the others listen silently. This is not always easy for those who have never experienced it, but over a few weeks the group can become a precious and holy place. Taking away the need to respond and the opportunity to interrupt makes way for a depth of listening that is seldom encountered. This is no small claim to make, but participants confirm it.

Initially for the sharer this can feel disconcerting, uncomfortable, exposing, frustrating, weird…but staying with this process of listening causes a growing recognition that when sharing one will be listened to and respected.

For the listener there is a growing appreciation of the sharer's humanity and faith with a sense of awe and compassion. The effect is a deep relationship among the group. This has profound effects in people and how they feel about themselves. They gain a growing sense that they have a place where they feel accepted, warts and all! For some this can be the only place they have found this. People grow in confidence to 'be more themselves' elsewhere, and are better able to share something of their faith in other less controlled situations. Thus these groups can be places where authentic evangelism (that is personal faith sharing) is nurtured and enabled.

Safe Space

Undergirding these three keys to spiritual growth is the provision of safe space. This is both physical and emotional. It is where threat is minimized with protection from intrusion and destructive behaviour and attitudes. This is the space that we believe God offers each of us, but which is too seldom recognized or appreciated. Sadly the church can often be a place where the sacredness of individual space is least honoured—often with the blindest of good intentions! We look at this in more detail in chapter 5, but at this stage it is worth pointing out some of the key features that aid creating safe space.

- Freedom from external interruption, so others are not likely to intrude into the space, nor are there major sources of external noise nearby.
- Freedom from internal interruption, so people within the group do not disturb one another by imposing their own agendas on others.
- Freedom from disrespect and abuse, through mutual acceptance and holding boundaries on responding and confidentiality.

4   Session Plans

These plans provide a detailed outline to each session with some commentary.

Further resources including more in-depth articles on the talks are available on the web site.

Session 1: Approaching Spirituality

The purpose of this session is to enable people to:

- Be welcomed and settle into the course.
- Tune into their own motivations and desires.
- Become aware of the love of God for them revealed in the Scripture passages.
- Clarify what 'spirituality' is.
- Gain some helpful guidance on how to approach exploring spirituality.

1 Welcome and Introductions

Begin by welcoming everyone and introducing the team. Then invite each person to reflect on why they have come and what their hopes are for the course. Ask them to turn to their neighbours, introduce themselves and share what they are comfortable with about their reasons for coming and their hopes. Finally invite them to share with the whole group. (There is no need for everyone to do this—just get a flavour of the group's responses.)

2 Introducing the Course

This short talk gives an outline of the course's structure and guidance on how best to approach the course.

Each evening has the same basic format:

- *Stilling:* to become more open to God.
- *Spiritual Exercise:* ways of letting ourselves receive from God.
- *Group Sharing:* listening to each other's experience; honouring each sharing with silence.

- *Reflections and Perspectives on Spiritual Life and Journeying:* ways of helping to make sense of and make connections between experience and faith.
- *Material to Take Home:* reminder of the session and ideas to explore further.

Helpful attitudes to seek as participants:

- Seeking to listen
- Being open to the Spirit of God and to possibilities, to let go and let God, dare to trust!
- Honouring yourself and others.
- Confidentiality
- Being prepared to journey…

3 Reflection

Give some time for people to reflect for themselves following these points.

- How do I feel about this?
- What do I seek/need from God to be able to do this?
- Share in pairs.
- Invite them to quietly pray for this (hold silent space for this).

4 Stilling

Introduce the process of the stilling time and the prayer exercise. Pass around the prayer handout, but ask them to put it to one side until after the stilling. Invite a deep breathing, a letting go, letting God…Then play a peaceful piece of music.

Further ideas for stilling and music to use are on the web site.

5 Spiritual Exercise

Letting Scripture Speak to Us: Lectio Divina (15 minutes)

- Read both passages slowly, then invite people to spend time with one of them.
- At the end invite people to jot down notes on their experience (three or four minutes).

This is a simple way into Lectio Divina—one of the oldest ways in the Christian tradition of praying with Scripture. This slow and gentle way of letting Scripture speak allows the dawning of new insights and the power of imagery that speak deep into hearts.

A helpful way of introducing people to this method is to invite people to listen quietly to the words—as if spoken personally to them, and to simply notice what strikes them as they listen. When something strikes them, to stay with it and let the impact of the word or phrase deepen and develop. It is not about taking every word in from the passage, rather a matter of being attentive to the particular words, phrases or images that, as it were, are for them.

6 Listening Groups

Listening to One Another (20–30 minutes)

- Divide into groups of no more than six which then go to their meeting places with group enablers.
- Once the group has gathered, the group enabler welcomes everyone and introduces them to the group process—handing out the guideline sheet.
- The group is then invited to reflect on this and then to introduce themselves to the group, sharing their hopes and fears about the group.
- The enabler then invites people to share reflections on their experience of the prayer exercise when they are ready.

7 Plenary

Receive some feedback from the group experience:

- How did that feel? How did it feel to share? To be listened to?

8 Input

Approaching Spirituality (10 minutes)

This talk offers insights on spirituality and encourages attentiveness—firstly by exploring spirituality as being that which sustains faith life, and then looking at helpful ways of paying attention to our own spiritual/inner life.

9 Conclusion

Invite participants to reflect further during the week ahead noticing what experiences brought love, joy, peace, faith, hope, life, and to record them in their notebooks.

Hand out the session card. There is a card for participants to take away at the end of each session. These are A6 in size and contain some pointers for reflection and prayer. We print them on different coloured card for each week.

Prayer and the Grace. A simple form of ending can be used. Do not use this to repeat points from the talk, rather just to affirm the need for God's grace to continue the journey.

Session 2: Getting to Know God Better/Faith Journeys

The purpose of this session is to enable people to:

- Connect their lived experience with the images of faith journey offered.
- Know every part of their journey is valuable.
- Hear and know God's invitation flowing through their lived experience.
- Affirm God's loving presence and action in all experiences.

1 Welcome

Welcome everyone and ask them to answer to themselves 'How are you?' Then invite them to share briefly in pairs. Remind the group that God is here and has brought us here, that God's purposes are to enable us to become more who we were created to be. Finally remind them that this becoming is helped by giving space and attention to our inner life—the space where God's Spirit is present and working.

2 Stilling and Relaxation

This stilling can be led by inviting people as they quieten to listen—firstly to the sounds they hear that are coming from outside, then from the inside of the building, and finally those of their own body. Then as they breathe in to seek to be drawing in the breath of God, and to let go of any tensions as they breathe out. Play gentle music to hold the stillness.

3 Reflection Exercise

Flower of Me

- Introduce: A time to reflect on life experience, to jot down notes or draw, in each of the petals, reminders of times in your life that fit the description.
- Second stage: Can you notice any connecting movements between the experiences on the different petals?

This exercise invites people to explore various kinds of life experiences and to look at them, noticing the movements of God in their life. The handout describes the process people are invited to follow. Insights and awarenesses that emerge can be significant and can be painful. Honouring what people share and their vulnerability is important. Equally, it is helpful to encourage them to recognize their inner longing for God and to find ways of giving time and attention to this.

4 Listening Groups

5 Feedback

> • Invite feedback from group experience asking: How was it to be listened to? Were there any striking awarenesses about listening and being listened to?

6 Input

Journeying with God

In this talk, the understanding of faith as a journey is explored. Here the uniqueness of each person's journey can be affirmed while recognizing there are many common features to faith journeys. Taking this further, the helpfulness of cyclical images (eg tides and seasons)[2] is explored, recognizing how they relate to our lives and the life of Jesus. Finally point out that faith takes us into new places and therefore brings both uncertainty and the invitation to trust God in new ways.

For further exploration of these themes, see the resources on the web site.

7 Conclusion

Hand out the card for this session, and then conclude with a prayer and the Grace.

Session 3: Who am I?

> The purpose of this session is to enable people to:
>
> • Become more aware of their identity as beloved of God.
> • Seek the treasure of God present within themselves.
> • Affirm that their inner desires and longings are important in this search.

1 Introduction

This is much as the previous session, concluding with a brief description of the session's theme 'Who am I?'

2 Stilling/Relaxation

Lead the group gently through a bodily relaxation—starting from the top of the head and moving through the body, unhurriedly, tensing and relaxing different parts. Conclude with playing some gentle music.

3 Imaginative Contemplation
Luke 19.1–10—Zacchaeus

> • This led imaginative contemplation should lead people into imagining the scene, finding their own place in it and enabling them to become personally involved as they are taken through the key moments of the scene.

This approach to prayer has a long history. It involves taking a gospel passage and seeking to imagine the scene, and be part of it, interacting with the characters and especially with Jesus. Often described as Ignatian Prayer, this approach predates him, but he used it extensively in the Spiritual Exercises. It enables deep personal engagement with Christ in prayer and can result in deeply transformed spiritual orientations. Some can find this a daunting way of prayer to approach because in early years they were told they had no imagination, or because they have come to distrust their imaginations. This can be helped by gentle encouragement, for example to assure people the only ability needed is to be able to picture rooms in their house. At the end of this time offer the Review of Prayer handout and give them a few minutes to reflect with it.

4 Listening Groups
5 Feedback

> • How did it feel to be listened to? Any striking awarenesses?

6 Input: Who am I?
This talk explores how identity can be seen in different aspects of life (for example job, status, feelings) which can undermine our appreciation of our true identity as children of God.[3] Encouragement to explore one's deeper or truer self is given with some suggestions of how to start doing this.

7 Final Reflection
Offer these points to the group.

> • Jot down any significant awarenesses that have emerged tonight.
> • Do not forget to look after yourself. If you find yourself emotionally stirred, give yourself time to name the feelings and reflect on what they may be telling you. It may be helpful to talk this through with someone.

8 Conclusion
Hand out the card for this session, the exercise 'Looking at ourselves' before concluding with a prayer and the Grace.

Session 4: Who is God to Me?

The purpose of this session is to enable people to:

- Connect their life experience with the nature of the movement of grace.
- Be aware of how images of God have affected their faith journey.
- Be more discerning in recognizing the images of God that may be influencing their lives.

1 Introduction

The now usual question 'How are you?' with brief sharing in pairs followed by a short description of the session's theme—Exploring our images of God.

2 Stilling/Relaxation

Lead the group by inviting them to be aware of the support of their body by their seat and the floor. As they become aware of this groundedness, remind them of the support of God, the ground of our being and encourage an inner sense of letting go to be supported, grounded and resting on God. Follow this with some relaxing music.

3 Praying with Rembrandt's Return of the Prodigal Son

This exercise is best done in small groups. The listening groups are the natural place with the Group Enabler leading the reflection using the points below. Obviously it is necessary to have a copy of the painting for each group.[4]

This painting speaks powerfully of God's loving, forgiving acceptance. Henri Nouwen spent a week gazing at the picture—all we offer is twenty minutes, with some simple prompts for attention and reflection.[5] As in all these exercises, the aim is to let God speak through it, rather than telling people what God is saying. Time needs to be given between the prompts for this reflection.

- Spend time with picture, let yourself be in the place of the son, a son or daughter enfolded in the hands of the father...
- Look at the face of the father—sense how he is looking at you, his child...
- Look at the hands of the father (one masculine, one feminine)—imagine them on your back...
- Receive the hold, love, acceptance of the father, who was not even interested in any prepared speech of apology...
- Stay with this until you feel you want to move on.

Give all but the last few minutes as space to be with the picture. Near the end of the time encourage the group to make some notes of their experience. Then offer the Window on God exercise to take away for further reflection.

The Window on God exercise invites reflection on the images of God that are important to us. It does this from the perspective of past and present experience as well as future hope and desire. Many significant awarenesses can emerge from this.

4 Listening Groups

5 Feedback

- Invite feedback from the listening group experience: how did it feel to be listened to? Have any striking awarenesses emerged about listening? Do the groups feel different now, compared to the first sessions?

6 Input

The Dynamic Cycle[6]

Frank Lake's Dynamic Cycle provides a means of looking at the way God's grace can be recognized in the way in which life is motivated. If offers a way of recognizing when forces are operating on our living that are harmful and separate us from the God of grace. This connects human experience with the life of Christ and the meaning of the cross in bringing God's hope and healing to a wounded world. The cycle becomes a valuable discerning tool, providing a way of noticing the contrasting effects of life motivated by grace and life driven by works.

7 Reflect

- Jot down any significant awarenesses that have emerged tonight.
- Do not forget to look after yourself, particularly if you find yourself emotionally stirred.

8 Conclusion

Hand out the card for this session and the exercise 'Healing our image of God' before concluding with the Grace.

Session 5: Called to Become

The purpose of this session is to enable people to:

- Find that the many facets of themselves (particularly those they are uncomfortable with) are welcomed by the love of God.
- Become aware of how they can discern God in their inner responses to experiences.

- Encourage responses to this discernment by seeking to move with the Spirit.

1 Introduction

As in previous sessions, with a brief outline of the session's theme—Discerning God's leading in my life.

2 Relaxation

Offer a simple led relaxation of becoming still, loosening the body, letting go of tension and the weights of the day and gently relaxing. Follow with music.

3 Banquet of Our Whole Selves

- Give out the handout and invite people to find a comfortable space to do this exercise.

This prayer exercise uses both reflection and imaginative prayer. The first part invites personal reflection on oneself and all that feels unacceptable. It invites honest self-awareness and then offers a way of praying with what has emerged.

> *Significant shifts in relationships with God happen through an encounter with the God who loves the unlovely*

The second part takes you, in imagination, to meet Jesus as the host of the banquet and to introduce to him the different unacceptable 'characters' you have identified.

This can be challenging and emotional, but ultimately healing and transforming. Significant shifts in relationships with God happen through an encounter with the God who loves the unlovely.

Probably the most powerful prayer exercise of the course, it can be helpful to encourage those who may have found it too difficult to cope with at the time to pray with this again at home.

4 Listening Groups

5 Feedback

It is likely there will be some comments about the difficulty of sharing when there are powerful emotions around. Simply acknowledge this. Given the depth this prayer exercise can take people to, it is helpful to affirm that God is at work, particularly when emotions are stirred. As has been said, tears are evidence of the Holy Spirit at work. Encourage those who may have found painful and difficult inner responses emerging to give themselves time with them. It is worth pointing out the value of having a supportive listener to give you space to talk about your experience.

6 Input

Co-operating with God

Discernment is an important yet often neglected dimension of faith and spirituality. One of the crucial questions about any spirituality is about how it helps discernment and informs the making of choices.

In this talk the importance of discernment in our choices is explored. Guidance based on Ignatius of Loyola's guidelines for the discernment of spirits is offered. These are looked at in the light of Paul's fruit of the Spirit in Galatians 5.

7 Reflection

- What has been striking, helpful...?
- What has been challenging, disturbing...?
- What do I need to do to care for myself?

8 Conclusion

Hand out the card for this session and the exercise 'Considering my life' before concluding in prayer.

Session 6: Where am I Going?—Journeying On...

The purpose of this session is to enable people to:

- Reflect on their faith journey and where it may be leading them.
- Become more aware of their 'dreams' for their life and the invitation from God that may be in it.
- To identify ways in which they can sustain their spiritual life beyond the course.
- Let go of the course and journey on.

1 Introduction

Begin as usual with the question 'How are you?' and the invitation to share this in pairs. Then read as a prayer Thomas Merton's prayer.[7]

2 Relaxation

3 Exercise

Time with the Poem 'I will dream a dream'[8]

- Invite people to notice what words, phrases, and lines strike them as they hear the poem read. Suggest they stay with the striking

word or phrase and let its meaning for them emerge.
- Read the poem.

This poem provides an excellent way into exploring where God may be calling each of us in our lives. It encourages awareness of the deep longings within which the clues to our vocation can be found.

4 Listening Groups

5 Feedback
It can be helpful to invite people to reflect on the journey of the listening groups. How has their feeling about the group changed over the course? What have they noticed and learnt about their sharing and their listening?

6 Input

Journeying On...
Offer a fairly brief talk on journeying onwards from the course with God. Invite reflection on what has been helpful from the course that they will be taking away with them. Then offer some ideas of how the journey onward can be supported and encouraged through the three keys to spiritual growth the course is founded on. Conclude by inviting personal pondering on what the 'dream of God' is that they may sense is calling them on.

Where Do I Go from Here?

- Ponder 'What is my dream?'
- Take a few minutes to do this—jot down any things that emerge.

7 Meditation with Blind Bartimeus
This time, of meditation, imaginative exercise and prayer, is a way of acknowledging the journey through Soul Spark, and to pray for where it may be leading. At the same time it is a letting go of the course, marking the end of a stage of the journey of faith and life. The setting of the space for this session involves having a central candle. Everyone is given a tea-light candle that at the end they bring forward, light and place around the central candle.

8 Conclusion
Give out the card for this session and then conclude with prayer and goodbyes.

Running Soul Spark 5

The Team

We believe the best way of running this course is with a team who facilitates the sessions and the groups. Not everyone in the team needs to carry the same responsibilities. There need to be sufficient gifts within the group to cover the tasks of co-ordination, leading sessions, giving inputs and facilitating the listening groups.

The team needs to be comprised of people who are open and attentive to their own spiritual journeys, and are comfortable with the experiential approach of the course. Without this, team members can undermine the effectiveness of the course, and, worse still, get in the way of God's work in participants.

Co-ordinator's Role

The co-ordinator has an important role in making the arrangements for the venue and drawing the team together. They will need to gather the team before the course to ensure the team are clear about how it works, what their role is, and to decide tasks. Team members can be used for more than just facilitating the listening groups. They can lead the stilling times, introduce prayer exercises and give the talks. They will need to ensure week by week that the team know what is happening and to arrange prayer time before and after each session and reflection and sharing time afterwards. Their own ongoing reflection on the process and progress of the course will be important.

It is worth selecting team members carefully, ensuring that they are comfortable with the approach and style of the course. It is helpful to get the team together before the course to get to know one another and talk through how it all will work. Investing time and energy in team building is important and worthwhile.

Investing time and energy in team building is important and worthwhile

There are networks from which team members may be drawn. Those offering Spiritual Direction or accompanying others on Weeks of Accompanied Prayer and Individually Guided Retreats may well be suitable team members. Contact details for networks and groups are listed on the web site.

This is a place to acknowledge reactions rather than trying to resolve them

Team times before and after each session are important. It is important that those who seek to enable others to be more open to God through this process support and encourage each other to do the same. So to pray together before each session and reflect afterwards gives a structure to this.

The time for reflection after each meeting gives each team member an opportunity to share how they found themselves reacting. This is a place to acknowledge reactions rather than trying to resolve them. The meeting can conclude with checking plans for the next session and prayer.

The team can develop good friendships from working together. We have held a meal together after the end of the course to help a good ending. These are times for both reflecting on the experience together and enjoying each other's company.

Environment

The environment is important. A room that feels comfortable and easy to relax in is likely to help people settle into the process more easily. It is worth looking at the following:

- External noise levels, to ensure that people can be heard easily
- Ensure the session will not be disturbed or interrupted.
- Comfortable seating and room temperature will help people settle
- Relaxed ambience—so it is easy for people to feel at ease

In addition it is helpful to create a visual focus for the space. We create these with candles, crosses, fabrics, water, stones, flowers, and so on. They have always attracted appreciative comments.

Creating Safe Space

The team running Soul Spark have a significant role in holding safe space in a way that makes it holy ground. Max Warren's description of the appropriate attitude to mission applies here:

Our first task in approaching another person, another people, another culture, another faith, is to take off our shoes for the place we are approaching is holy. Else we may find ourselves treading on another's dream. More serious still, we may forget that God was there before our arrival.[9]

Holding safe space is like being a plant pot! The pot holds what is helpful for growth, and excludes that which is unhelpful. The team holds helpful and appropriate boundaries, within which people feel secure and free to be with whatever they find within themselves. The prayer exercises, the sharing and the inputs, provide valuable water, fertilizer and supports for the growth that God brings about, to happen as freely as possible.

Maintaining boundaries prevents:
- The distraction of other people's agendas
- Judgmental comments
- Inappropriate responses
- Distracting interruptions

As already acknowledged, there is personal challenge in taking on this role. Holding a process where the intention is to honour other people's journeys and not interfere can confront us with our own struggles. We can be faced with our own weaknesses and woundedness, with the temptation to solve problems, control, manipulate and interfere. It is crucial for leaders to recognize this and to be able to notice when their own 'stuff' may be coming into play. When it does, to acknowledge this to themselves, put it to one side and keep focused. Afterwards they can take time to look at what was going on and prayerfully seek God's grace.

Leading the Prayer Times

This is an art rather than a science! The leading of the whole group in prayer involves a sensitive balance between clear leading and light holding. The leader needs to hold the space and offer a focus so that each person is able to engage freely with God. This raises questions of pace, language and the space for individual experience.

The leader needs to hold the space and offer a focus so that each person is able to engage freely with God

The imaginative contemplation and the reflections on the Rembrandt painting in Sessions 3 and 4 need to be led so people have enough time to ponder each point before moving on to the next. Personal experience of helpful pacing is an important aid for judging this. As a rough rule of thumb we suggest leaving gaps about twice as long as might be felt appropriate—this can counterbalance any nerves that cause rushing!

The language used can help or hinder. It is important to use open language, saying things in ways that invite, are open to possibilities and gives a sense of personal freedom. Avoid absolute language and anything that implies value-judgment or makes assumptions about how people will react. Consider the difference between these two sentences that might be used in leading through the story of Zacchaeus.

'You feel embarrassed as Jesus looks at you.'
'How does it feel as Jesus looks at you?'

The first imposes a feeling on the listener; the second invites them to be aware of their own feeling. Doing this all involves giving space to the participants, and leaves the leader with the privilege of not knowing what is happening! Accept the discomfort of this and trust that God knows!

Facilitating the Listening Groups

Put simply the guidelines for the listening groups are:

- Each person need share only what they are comfortable with sharing.
- Everyone simply listens to the sharing of the others without any verbal response.
- What is heard is confidential and is not repeated or raised outside the group except by the person who shared.

The unusual nature of the listening group process can make the role of group enabler more challenging than might be expected. There can be discomfort in the group in the first couple of sessions as people settle into it. Enablers need to be prepared for this and hold to the process. There can be a strong temptation or pull towards other more common group processes, and this needs to be held in check.

There are two important reasons for this group process. First, it protects sharers from comeback that can hurt and damage when they are making themselves vulnerable. Secondly, it is easy for responses to move the focus away from that of the sharer. Experience has shown that by minimizing these factors, the space becomes a place where not only are you 'heard into speech,' but discerning God becomes much easier.

The enabler can easily feel superfluous when a group has started to settle into the process, because they do not seem to be 'doing anything'! Mostly their role is one of presence. By being there they 'hold the process' and over time have the privilege of beholding the work of God in people's lives. Again there is the need simply to accept the discomfort of feeling unneeded and trust that God is doing what is necessary.

Having said this there is more value than is often appreciated in doing what is asked of them in the role of group facilitator:

24

- At the first session introduce the group to the process and invite commitment to it.
- At the beginning of the next couple of sessions remind the group of the guidelines.
- Mark the end of the group time when everyone who wants to has shared. Thank everyone for their sharing and listening, and perhaps encourage ongoing honouring one another by entrusting to God all that has been shared and heard.
- Gently intervene if at any time the guidelines to the process are being overstepped.

The groups work best with a consistent membership. Trust and openness grows and the sharing deepens and the value of the group is appreciated. We have known some groups continue to meet to listen to each other long after the course has finished.

Resources for Participants

As part of the welcome on the first night we provide a plastic 'polywallet' with a notebook, pen and the first night's handouts inside. This does not cost much and gives people a sense that their needs are being cared for and resourced.

We have had to adapt the materials, on occasion, to suit particular needs. A blind person needed other ways of engaging with the written and visual exercises. We record the words onto cassette and provide a personal stereo for a blind person. For someone with hearing difficulties we used a loop system. A little imagination and effort is all that is necessary!

Handling Issues that Arise

Opening to God and others can feel risky and dangerous. Gentle handling can help these difficulties become places of grace and growth! Below we explore some of the common issues that may emerge.

Difficulties in Listening Groups

It is important to encourage the sharing of doubts and anxieties in the feedback time after the sharing groups. Two types of struggle almost always emerge. Very private people find it hard to share and very extrovert people find it hard to not respond. It is worth assuring the group that these struggles are normal and understandable and encouraging them to hold to the process through the discomfort and see what happens. There is often a threshold of trust to cross and this can take time. The group facilitator can help by gently reminding the group of the guidelines each week and by being an encouraging presence.

Difficult or Uncomfortable 'Stuff' Coming Up

What is stuff? This is a useful shorthand term for emotional reactions that are uncomfortable and difficult to handle. At the end of each session participants are encouraged to take care of themselves, to take seriously what is emerging and trust that it is coming up for healing. It is helpful to encourage taking time for further reflection and prayer. Often the prayer 'Lord show me' and some quiet reflection is helpful. There may not be a quick answer, but living with it can become easier. It can also be helpful to find someone to share and reflect with—someone who will listen rather than try to fix it for them.

Struggles to be Still

Acknowledge that it can be hard to be still. Finding stillness is not easy and being distracted is common. Encouraging people to stay with it and relax can help to settle into it over the weeks. See 'Ways of helping stillness' from the web resources for further ideas on this.

Struggles to Engage with Prayer

Each prayer exercise will have its fans and its critics. For those who struggle with an exercise it can be worth encouraging them to look at why this is. Some will struggle because they want to get it right and feel they cannot do it. It is good to affirm diversity and acknowledge struggles. A gentle reminder that prayer is not about 'doing it right' but about seeking to be open to the Spirit can help a lot. They may need encouragement to reflect on their inner attitudes to the prayer and see if they are getting in the way. The 'Reviewing Prayer' handout can be helpful for this. It is worth noting that some of the most important experiences in prayer are when we are struggling and feeling we are failing. Usually the gift of this can be hard to recognize, emerging only as it is spoken about.

Where Next?

The participants' journey continues beyond Soul Spark and is not dependent on it! Many have a sense of something rich emerging for them and therefore want to keep this going. They can feel slightly panicky about losing what has started and wonder 'what's next' or 'how do I keep this going?'

This process of prayer, faith sharing and listening is one that can be continued in many ways, within a group or individually. Providing information on what is happening locally will be appreciated as will information on finding supports like Spiritual Direction, events like quiet days, retreats and spirituality workshops.

It may be that they have found the need for further support during the course and discovered the value of the safe listening place. This could be one of the ways ahead for them.

It is not uncommon for group enablers to find they are anxious about how some members of their groups will manage after Soul Spark. They need to find ways of letting go; processing these feelings and prayerfully handing them over to God.

Evaluation

At the end we invite participants to complete and return an evaluation sheet. It has been a deep privilege to see where Soul Spark has taken people and what has been received. The evaluation sheet also offers a way for people to express any difficulties they have encountered. For some the course is not easy and they need a chance to express this. The resulting feedback needs to be reflected on with the same discerning spirit the course has encouraged. There are usually things said that need simply to be noted, while others need to be learnt from.

Final Word 6

Soul Spark has been an evolving journey.

Each time we have run it we have found new insights and perspectives emerging, both on the material we share as well as in the way we run it. Each time we have run it has resulted in some refinement and development.

We now offer it for further evolution, out of our hands and into yours. We hope and pray that it will be used to enable more people to deepen their awareness of their spirituality and value attending to it.

The task of putting down in writing what the course involves has been a challenging task. There is so much that could have been said, but which cannot be squeezed into this booklet. If you find yourself drawn to offer the course, but needing clarification, please get in touch. We welcome your enquiries, feedback and discussion of issues arising from running Soul Spark via the web site.

May the God of life bless your using this material.

Bibliography

We recommend these books, in addition to those referenced in the notes, as useful reading to accompany the course.

Angela Ashwin, *Patterns not Padlocks* (Eagle, 2002)
Joyce Huggett, *Listening to God* (Hodder and Stoughton, 1996)
Joyce Huggett, *Listening to Others* (Hodder and Stoughton, 1996)
Gerard W Hughes, *God of Surprises* (Darton, Longman and Todd, 1985)
Dennis Linn, Sheila Fabricant Linn, Matthew Linn, *Good Goats: Healing Our Image of God* (Paulist Press, 1994)
Dennis Linn, Sheila Fabricant Linn, Matthew Linn, *Sleeping with Bread* (Paulist Press, 1995)
Ronald Rolheiser, *Seeking Spirituality* (Hodder and Stoughton, 1998)
Margaret Silf, *Taste and See* (Darton, Longman and Todd, 1999)
Gerald O'Mahoney, *Finding the Still Point* (Eagle, 2002)
Anthony de Mello, *Sadhana* (Bantam Doubleday Dell, 1984)
Philip Yancey, *What's So Amazing About Grace?* (Zondervan, 2002)

Notes

1 The Spiritual Exercises of St Ignatius of Loyola, Annotation 15.
2 David Adam, *Tides and Seasons* (SPCK, 1982) provides a helpful exploration of this.
3 Margaret Silf, *Landmarks* (Darton, Longman and Todd, 1998); chapter 1 offers a helpful model for understanding our sense of identity.
4 Large reproductions of this can be obtained from Pauline Books and Media www.pauline-uk.org or Christian bookshops.
5 Henri Nouwen, *The Return of the Prodigal Son* (Darton, Longman and Todd, 1994).
6 The Dynamic Cycle from Frank Lake, *Clinical Theology* (Darton, Longman and Todd, 1986) forms the foundation for this way into exploring images of God. The web resources include a detailed description of this and a handout. David Runcorn, *Touch Wood* (Darton, Longman and Todd, 1992) has a helpful chapter on this.
7 The prayer we use here is the one that begins 'Lord, I have no idea where I am going...' The full text is available with the web resources.
8 This poem by French writer Charles Péguy is quoted in Gerard Hughes, *God in All Things* (Darton, Longman and Todd, 2003).
9 The Reverend Doctor Max Warren, General Secretary of the Church Missionary Society 1942–1962.